SACRED
INTIMACY

Books by Brenton G. Yorgason and/or Blaine M. Yorgason

Sacred Intimacy****
Little Known Evidences of the Book of Mormon
Decision Point
Pardners — Three Stories on Friendship
In Search of Steenie Bergman (Soderberg Series #5)
KING — A Biography of Jerome Palmer King
The Greatest Quest
Seven Days for Ruby (Soderberg Series #4)
Family Knights****
The Eleven-Dollar Surgery
Becoming
Bfpstk and the Smile Song***
The Shadow Taker**
The Loftier Way: Tales From the Ancient American Frontier
Brother Brigham's Gold (Soderberg Series #3)
Ride the Laughing Wind
The Miracle
The Thanksgiving Promise (paperback — movie version)
Chester I Love You (paperback — movie version)
Chester I Love You (Soderberg Series #2)
Double Exposure
Seeker of the Gentle Heart
The Krystal Promise
A Town Called Charity, and Other Stories about Decisions
The Bishop's Horse Race (Soderberg Series #1)
The Courage Covenant (Massacre at Salt Creek)
Windwalker (movie version)
The Windwalker
Others
Charlie's Monument
From First Date to Chosen Mate
Tall Timber
Miracles and the Latter-day Saint Teenager
From Two to One*
From This Day Forth*
Creating a Celestial Marriage (textbook)*
Marriage And Family Stewardships (textbook)*

*Coauthored with Wesley R. Burr and Terry R. Baker
**Coauthored with Carl J. Eaton
***Coauthored with Tami B. Yorgason
****Coauthored with Margaret Yates Yorgason

SACRED INTIMACY

BRENTON AND MARGARET
YORGASON

Deseret Book Company
Salt Lake City, Utah

Library of Congress Cataloging-in-Publication Data

Yorgason, Brenton G.
    Sacred intimacy / by Brenton G. and Margaret Yorgason.
       p. cm.
    ISBN 0-87579-273-1
    1. Intimacy (Psychology) — Religious aspects — Christianity.
2. Marriage — Religious aspects — Mormon Church. 3. Mormon Church —
Doctrines. 4. Church of Jesus Christ of Latter-day Saints —
Doctrines. I. Yorgason, Margaret. II. Title.
BX8641.Y684 1989
248.8′44 — dc20   89-38391
                                                      CIP

Printed in the United States of America

10   9   8   7   6   5   4   3   2   1

For Wes and Ruth

Contents

Acknowledgments

We wish to thank the following friends and family who made suggestions that have improved this book: Lew and Marilyn Kofford, Gerald and Betty Owen, Gayle and Lucy Yorgason, Art and Dallas Berg, Blaine and Kathy Yorgason, Dave and Sheila Zolman, Rick and Shauna Brown, Jeff and Pat England, Gary and Lannie Garcia, Marty and Deanna Ehman, Craig and Patti Alder, Dick and Sharleen Thomas, Ron and Beth Spotten, Floyd and Kathy Bird, Bob and Lori Nielson, Van and Donna Midgley, Bob and Sue Weeks, Jim and Analee Mickelson, and John and Linda Rich.

We would also like to give special thanks to Sheri Dew, a friend and associate, for her editorial assistance on this book.

Introduction

Isn't it great to be in love! We've never been so much in love. After twenty-two years, our relationship just gets better. And while we've had our share of ups and downs, from frustrations associated with rearing children to the other challenges of daily living, our marriage has not only held together but has become stronger and richer with time.

When we first considered writing a book for couples, our focus was on the need for husbands and wives to experience appropriate and fulfilling sexual intimacy. Perhaps the most predictive barometer for marital success and stability is the quality of a couple's physical relationship. But interestingly, this seems to also be the first area where things can go wrong. Though there are many reasons for sexual dysfunction and dissatisfaction, when sexual intimacy is lacking the marriage usually suffers.

As a consequence, we determined to focus our writing on this very important facet of marriage.

But as we began to develop our ideas and thoughts into book format, we realized that, while being extremely important in marriage, the sexual union is only one of at least five facets of intimacy in a relationship. We began to realize how interrelated they all are, and how important to the health and progression of any relationship are all areas of intimacy: nonverbal, verbal, emotional, physical, and spiritual. Physical intimacy in marriage, as important as it is, is shallow until elevated to the position the Lord intended. At that point it becomes a very powerful, important facilitator to furthering emotional and spiritual bonding.

Then, as we explored things further, we came to believe that this book could have meaningful application to all adults, regardless of marital status, because the same principles that will help a couple achieve complete intimacy in their marriage also apply to the development of all significant interpersonal relationships. And how important are they? The quality of our significant relationships adds to the richness and fullness of life.

So wherever you are at this point in life, whatever your circumstances are, we hope this book will have meaning to you.

Obviously, the most enduring and significant relationship is the marriage relationship. Because it embraces all facets of intimacy, this book focuses on that specific union.

What is intimacy? By definition, it is the compelling desire and need to be linked to, or to be connected with, another person.

We all long for intimacy—to touch and be touched, to listen to and be listened to, to care for and be cared for, to love and be loved. The difference between a life that is rich with color or empty and hollow depends on our ability to sustain and develop close, intimate relationships.

Unfortunately, there aren't many of us who come by the skills required to develop close relationships naturally. Many come from homes where intimate relationships were not modeled by parents. Those individuals, in a sense, must play catch-up in trying to learn the skills that will help them be close to others. Whether you grew up in such an environment, or were privileged to have had parents who modeled these skills for you, we invite you to consider the contents of this book—to better understand and learn the skills that will give you meaningful interchange with those persons who are closest to you and who mean the most to you. One of the greatest skills we can learn in mortality is how to truly be close to others.

Just as a diamond is multifaceted, so is a good relationship. Just as the most beautiful diamonds are those that respond to pressure in the most productive and brilliant way, so are the most beautiful relationships those that, over time and with much hard work, respond well to the forces around them.

Once a diamond is formed, it becomes nearly impenetrable. Likewise, if a couple can achieve the brilliance of well-rounded, multifaceted intimacy, while difficult times may still come, there's little that can chip away at or damage the relationship.

As it turns out, falling in love is the easy part. It's after the honeymoon that we put on our work clothes and set out to shape the diamond of our relationship by developing the various facets in their fullest sense.

We hope that you will sense the spirit in which this book has been written. We do not see ourselves as having the final word, nor do we represent the Church in the things we share. We are simply two partners who believe deeply in the potential and sanctity of the marriage relationship and who believe that strong relationships don't just happen. We must learn how to make them happen.

May we suggest an approach to using this book? If possible, read these pages *together* with your spouse. As you do this, when one of you reads or hears something you'd like to discuss further, speak up and say so. Stop at that moment and share your feelings and perceptions until both of you are fully satisfied with the exchange. Be as honest yet as gentle as possible. Then proceed.

Finally, then, our hope is that this reading experience will become a springboard for you, as a couple, to explore more deeply the facets of your own marriage.

1

Verbal Intimacy

"Rejoice with the wife of thy youth."
(Proverbs 5:18.)

Part One

The time is the late 1800s, the place is the newly constructed meetinghouse in Ephraim, Sanpete County, Utah. The setting is the wedding ceremony for two young Scandinavian immigrants, performed perfunctorily by an aged bishop who barely speaks English but who is doing his best to capture the appropriate spirit for this occasion.

"Brodders and sisters . . . ."

His plow-calloused hands caressing the white pine finish of the new pulpit, the bishop surveyed the congregation with satisfaction and pride. Even to the three-sided galleries, the new meetinghouse was filled to overflowing.

It was good to be meeting in a house of worship outside the fort. Since 1854, Fort Ephraim had mothered the colony, but its inhabitants could not stay forever walled up in a rock enclosure—men, women, children, dugouts, covered wagons, corrals, chicken coops, chickens, a church (at first only cedar posts stuck into the ground), and a school. At night, flocks and herds were driven into the fort for protection until it was safe to corral them outside.

Having made their first tentative excursions out of the protection and close confinement of the fort to build this house of worship, the people were grateful to now have what seemed an oasis of rest for both body and soul.

Here it was that the great events of life were commemorated. Today the congregation had gathered for a wedding (and

1

if the English language suffered a few casualties with this Scandinavian bishop, worse things had happened).

"Brodders and sisters," the bishop repeated. "Ve air accumulated here today to behold von of da most sacred ordinances it is within our power to do. Ve has before us da vedding ceremony of Brodder Yon Yacob Yorgensen and Helena Sophina Turkelsen. . . . You young people up dere in the gallery!" the bishop suddenly interrupted. (There were members present who did not appreciate the gravity of the occasion.) "You vill please to produce no noise!

"Now," he resumed, "if da congregation vill please come to attention, Brodder Yon Yacob and Sister Helena Sophina, you vill please come up here to dis pulpit."

"Now, Brodder Yon Yacob Yorgensen, please take Sister Helena Sophina Turkelsen by da right hand. No, not shake hands, yust hold hands!

"So now, before dis congregation, and before all da Holy Angels do you Yon Yacob, take Helena Sophina for your vife? Do you promise dat you vill be a good, kind, loving and attentive husband? You say you vill?

"Brodders and sisters, he say he vill."

"And now, Sister Helena Sophina Turkelsen . . . yust keep hold of da hand! Do you promise dat you vill take Yon Yacob Yorgensen for your husband and dat you vill be a good, kind, and loving vife vhen he is sick, vell or hard to get along vith? You say you vill?" "Brodders and sisters, she say she vill."

"So now, if dere is anyone in dis congregation dat has any obyections to dis ceremony, vill you now speak up or forever shut up and mind your own business?

"Dere being no obyections, so now do I, da duly constituted bishop of Fort Ephraim, before dis congregation and before all da Holy Angels, and vith all da authority I has under my vest, I pronounce you father and mother." (True account taken from Grace Johnson, *Brodders and Sisters,* Messenger-Enterprise, Inc., Manti, Utah, 1973, pages 32-33.)

It is probable that these instructions were all that were given to these young newlyweds. It is likely too that, after a day or so honeymooning, this couple began to toil sixteen to eighteen hours a day in an attempt to support their new family. It is also likely that over the years they fell into the habit of seldom articulating their feelings about their marriage, let alone reading and learning how to improve their relationship with each other.

Much has taken place during the one hundred years since this couple was naively pronounced "Father and Mother" — and within the passing of these years a society has evolved wherein we can and oftimes must talk about aspects of marriage as well as our expectations about achieving true intimacy with our marriage partner.

Contrast the standard marriage beginnings of yesteryear with the thoughts shared by one woman who reflects on her experience with marital intimacy and the crucial role of sharing feelings and expectations:

> There are several reasons why our marriage, as well as the quality of intimacy within our marriage, is so good. The first is because we have been open in talking about our feelings, frustrations, what we like and don't like, etc. At first it was not easy for me to be so open; but through continually trying, patience, understanding, and time, it has become easier. Now, after almost thirty years, it is just second nature to me.
>
> Another reason is that my dear husband has always, without exception, been very thoughtful of my feelings. From our first night together, he has let my feelings be the determining factor; and from that first night I have felt that I could honestly express my feelings. Because he has been so thoughtful of me, it has created an "unvicious" cycle. I try harder to please him, and he tries harder to be considerate of me. The sexual part of our marriage has "perpetuated" itself, so to speak, because of our desire to please and help each other.
>
> A third reason we have had such success is because of

a little gimmick we adopted somewhere along the line which we call "donation." If I'm not as interested in closeness, then I can be as passive as I feel like being during our moment of intimacy—and this response (or lack of it) doesn't create threatening feelings inside him. Often it can start out with me being passive, but it doesn't always end that way. Because of his gentle, loving ways, I end up being as involved as he is. And too, there are times when my husband is the passive partner, and where he responds to my needs for an intimate expression of my love for him.

While this example centers around physical intimacy, it also demonstrates the crucial nature of verbal intimacy—being able to really talk with your partner.

One couple illustrates the importance of sharing feelings to increase the intimacy in their marriage:

> Number one, we talk! We are very open about what we are feeling, both emotionally and physically. We have always tried to communicate in our marriage, and we feel it is vitally important. If we haven't had answers and solutions on our own, we have sought professional help from doctors and counselors. It is so important to try to keep all questions answered and problems worked out, and not to be afraid to seek outside advice, if such advice is necessary.
>
> Number two, we are accommodating! Let us explain why it is important to us. Sometimes one of us is "not in the mood" to express love, however the other has a need to be fulfilled. This situation is not abused or taken unfair advantage of. It is important to fill the needs of our partners any way we can, whenever we can. It is also important for the partner in need to be understanding of the accommodating partner by realizing that this partner is rending unselfish love.
>
> We have been married almost eighteen years, and we know our relationship will continue to grow because we both work at it.

Part Two

The following is one of our favorite poems:

CLOUD NINE
Why is it
whenever I reach for the sky
to climb aboard cloud nine,
it evaporates and rains
upon my dreams?
Is it a matter of science,
or simply a matter of fact,
that not even a cloud
with a silver lining
can hold the weight of our dreams
    without some precipitation?
I think I've found the answer
to this dilemma—
Keep on reaching for the sky,
but don't forget your umbrella.
                Susan Stephenson

We all have "umbrella moments" in our marriages. Margaret remembers one such experience:

> In 1977, during the first semester of Brent's doctoral studies, he learned about the principle of "sharing feelings" within marriage. The idea of sharing feelings in a formal setting seemed risky to him, even though he was sure that our marriage did not need such mechanical instructions, for it had seemed almost perfect during the first ten years of our being together.

> But as he left class that day, Brent decided he would carefully select a moment to "check out" my feelings about what he perceived to be a near-perfect relationship.

> That evening, after our five children were successfully tucked in bed, he indicated that he wanted to have a special moment of sharing with me. We went into our family room, prepared a roaring fire in the fireplace, turned on the stereo, and then climbed confidently beneath the blanket on our sofa, each unaware of the marvelous though earth-shattering experience we would have in the next hour.

> Taking me into his arms, Brent held me briefly and silently. Then, pulling back and looking into my eyes, he asked

the question he had learned that day in class. "Honey," he whispered, "how do you *feel* about our marriage? Not what do you think about it, because I think I know that. I am interested in getting below the surface of your thoughts to explore your feelings about us."

For a brief moment I looked at him, my mind reeling with the impact of his question. I then did something that even I did not anticipate (something Brent had already learned was mine and every other woman's prerogative — to do the unexpected). I clouded up in about ten seconds and began to rain tears that turned into a torrential downpour. It is my memory (though it may not have happened exactly like this) that Brent got up, grabbed a bucket, and hurried and put it beneath my chin so the sofa would not become sopping wet.

About ten minutes later, after what had seemed an eternity, my tears gradually stopped. I then whispered my response.

"Brent, I'm so lonely! You are busy in your doctoral studies, with your bishopric work, and in spending endless hours counseling others at the drop of a hat, not to mention the time you spend reading and watching sports on television. But I spend my life talking to children, doing dishes and loads of wash and changing diapers. I just can't take it anymore. I need to know that you know I'm alive. I need you to talk to me!"

There, I had said it. Brent was stunned. I don't remember the balance of our conversation, except for the conclusion. Mustering strength, Brent announced the challenge the instructor had given in his class earlier that day.

"Margaret," he sighed, "why don't we set aside some time tomorrow night for sharing feelings. We can continue that routine for as long as we need to."

I smiled appreciatively, knowing how difficult it was for Brent to make such a commitment. I then agreed to his suggestion, and before I knew what was happening he whisked me off to bed and to my dreams.

Little did I understand the fear in Brent's mind. He had no idea what feelings we could talk about each night, even if it was for only a few minutes! For me, though, the prospect of getting to talk with Brent and actually share feelings each night gave me more optimism than I can now describe. I'll have to admit that I spent the next day wondering if we would actually follow through with our commitment to each other. I shouldn't have worried, however, for when 10:00 P.M. arrived we were nestled under our electric blanket, facing each other with anxious but determined smiles upon our faces.

That second sharing session was awkward, as was the third. Gradually, though, we found that our time of expressing feelings expanded to fill twenty minutes, then a full hour. We were both amazed at how much there was to talk about once the initial effort and commitment had been made. While our first conversations were limited and even superficial sometimes, they became effortless and very pleasurable interchanges over time.

Brent remembers the events as they unfolded: "After a couple of weeks of our nightly conversations, we changed the rules. We determined that from then on we would respond to each other's desire to share feelings when the need arose. Because Margaret is usually the one with the need to share feelings and emotions, as opposed to my inclination to watch another game, to wash the car, to read another chapter in a book, or to just spend time with the kids, she is usually the one who initiates discussion.

"If Margaret has such a need, she searches me out. The rule is that whatever I am doing, it is my responsibility to respond to her need to talk. Usually when she finds me, I notice a rain cloud gathering over her head, signalling her frame of mind. Our agreement is that I stop whatever I am doing, make eye and body contact, and make every effort to really listen as she expresses her feelings. She then takes whatever time she needs, and if I have listened well I usually end the conversation by rescuing her from a home filled with nine overpowering children. I've found it absolutely amazing how much a little support and energy on my part smooths out her temporary waters of despair."

Margaret found that verbally sharing feelings led to other positive developments in marriage:

"Even though both Brent and I are far from being perfect in this area, our ability to share feelings has increased immeasurably since that first rain-filled cloudburst. When we were newlyweds, we communicated quite well, but as children came along we gradually found ourselves communicating less and less.

"Falling into the vacuum of not speaking is a matter of natural course as a couple sets up housekeeping and the division of responsibility takes place. Each partner becomes somewhat consumed by his or her roles. But feelings are the substance of a marriage, and if they are not shared a barrier is gradually created. Now, however, as we share regularly, I find that my feelings of frustration don't build up as they did before. I used to let them stay inside until I felt as though I would pop like a firecracker.

"One of my favorite cartoons dealing with marriage is that of a wife glaring at her husband while he slouches in his easy chair, watching television. He states simply, 'I know we don't communicate. That's one of my few pleasures!' I laugh at that cartoon now, but there was a day in our marriage when I honestly felt like that lonely wife in the cartoon."

Not long ago we shared this experience with some friends whose marriage has had difficult moments stemming from a very difficult beginning. Upon hearing about our "umbrella day, " she said: "You talk as though a little rain is a downpour. For us, it has been one hurricane or cyclone or earthquake after another. Now, as we look back over twenty years of such massive storms of upheaval, we wonder if we have the energy or the ability to pick up the pieces."

We understand that, like ourselves, some couples only experience mild spring showers, while others weather torrential downpours. It is miraculous that this couple, as well as others like them, are still married. They have had many opportunities to be "blown away" by hurricanes and cyclones of conflict. If you are one of these couples, we commend you for weathering your storms and for being emotionally strong enough at this time to examine the quality of your marriage.

We have described a pivotal moment in our relationship with the hope that you will be encouraged to make a commitment to share your feelings with your companion. Perhaps reading and talking about the ideas presented in these pages will seem a bit too risky. But we believe that you will be pleasantly surprised at the results as you begin to really talk with each other and share feelings.

These days most of our talk time deals with thoughts and things that are happening all around us — everything from Jennifer's dental appointment and Joshua's grades to the pipe that froze in the kitchen and the gas level in the car. Many of our conversations deal with the surface-level issues it takes to keep a family going.

These areas of family management are vital to keep a marriage running smoothly. But couples need to regularly dive below the surface and share on the feeling level. Emotions are such a vital part of life and of marriage. Without feelings, a marriage would be like a black-and-white television. On the other hand, sharing feelings brings color and depth to the marriage picture. While the process may sound easy, it can take a concerted effort to risk and to share, even with your closest friend, your marriage partner.

Each of us has brought different communicating skills into marriage, skills or behavior patterns we likely learned by the example we had in our own homes as children. If your partner grew up in a home where his or her parents did not often express themselves, then you may feel as though you are pulling teeth to get a response from that partner.

Then, too, is the issue of timing.

Margaret explains: "I have found that timing is a vital aspect of communicating. For instance, when Brent is watching a BYU game with the children, I can be certain that he will not appreciate a deep sharing exchange with me. I try to be sensitive to the situation and wait for a better time to unload my heart."

Learning to label your emotions, or feelings, is a crucial skill that will allow you to be more expressive with your partner. You can acquire this skill by learning to identify your feelings, consider the words to describe them, and then share them with your spouse.

Below is a list of feelings that you can consider which will facilitate the verbal intimacy in your marriage. They are in the form of direct statements as well as metaphors:

Direct Statements

"I'm angry."
"I think I feel lonely tonight."
"I feel so excited that . . . "
"It is depressing to . . . "
"I feel sad about . . . "
"Deep inside I have a feeling of . . . "

Metaphors

"I feel like something the dog dragged in."
"I feel like I'm floating on a cloud."
"I feel like I'm carrying the whole world."
"I'm tingling all over."
"I feel like I'm ten feet tall."

In learning to verbalize feelings, the objective is for your partner to understand just what it is you are experiencing. One effective way to communicate is to use "I" statements. These are very different from "You" statements and "I-You" statements, and are especially helpful when expressing negative feelings where a partner is involved.

In the following three examples, consider how much better the "I" statements reflect a healthy marriage:

I statement: "I'm furious."

I-You statement: "I'm furious and it's your fault."
You statement: "You've made me furious."

I statement: "I'm so angry with this mess that I could scream!"
I-You statement: "I'm so mad at what you've done I could tear this place apart!"
You statement: "You've ruined the whole evening with this mess!"

I statement: "I feel as though I'm useless and unimportant."
I-You statement: "It hurts me when you don't come home on time or don't call."
You statement: "You don't even care about me, or how I feel."

It is obvious that the "I" statement has some strong advantages over the other forms of verbal expressions. It very clearly identifies your feelings, and it creates ownership. By using an "I" statement you communicate that the feeling exists and that it is inside you. It is your feeling. The other great advantage of an "I" statement is that it shows that you accept the responsibility for the feeling.

For your partner, hearing you express an "I" statement leaves him or her undefensive and thus more able to learn about your feeling. That in turn helps him or her better respond to it.

One skill we, as a couple, have attempted to learn over the years is that when one of us is upset, we try to separate our partner from the problem and thus leave their self-esteem unaffected.

Margaret says: "If Brent is upset with an overdrawn checkbook of mine, he is careful to let me know that he is upset with the situation and is not angry with me. I can handle that without falling apart."

Brent explains: "Margaret has actually led out as the example in responding verbally to unsettling moments. She always allows my self-esteem to remain intact simply by blaming the situation rather than attacking me personally.

"An example of her behavior took place not long ago when her car stopped, unannounced, and she had to walk several blocks home in a snowstorm. She could have easily attacked me for not having the carburator repaired, as I had planned on doing. But she didn't. She simply announced that the car was up on a certain corner, stated her frustration with not being home to have dinner ready, and then said she would be happy to go with me to help tow it down to the service station.

"At that moment I felt a sense of added security in my role of transportation provider, even though I had not done well, simply because I was unthreatened in my stewardship."

Part Three

On the surface, we might consider it ideal if we lived in a world where only positive experiences and feelings existed. Such an environment would not be conducive to growth and progression, however. We each need to learn how to deal with difficult situations and then how to come to grips with negative experiences and feelings. Learning to verbally express these negative feelings can actually become an art. While most of us in this life will not gain Picasso-like perfection, the following guidelines can assist us in achieving verbal intimacy:

Guidelines for Dealing with Negative Feelings

1. Is the "total environment" right? Check out the time of day, distractions, noise, privacy, outside pressures in the home, and so forth. In other words, strategize in your mind the appropriate time and place to express your feelings.

2. Ask yourself, "Am I in control?" Intense feelings may interfere with what your righteous objective should be. Therefore, if you feel that you are too emotional to express your feelings, you may decide to privately vent your intense feelings

first so that when you do express them to your spouse the results will bear fruit.

3. Ask yourself, "Is my partner in a mood to be receptive?" Is your spouse defensive, preoccupied, tired, or overworked. Preface your comments by asking: "Where are you now?" "Can I share a feeling?"

4. Remember: Be careful, sensitive and slow. Use tact, love, and consideration as you share your feelings and don't dump too much at once. If your partner becomes less receptive or defensive, wait until the proper mood can be recreated.

5. Be sure to include yourself in the problem. Almost all problems that cause intense negative feelings between partners are the result of interaction between them rather than from a single partner's actions. Use "I" statements. The resolution of your feelings will then almost magically take place.

6. Afterward, show an increase in love and tenderness.

Until now in our discussion of creating verbal intimacy in marriage, we have concentrated on the role of the expressor, or the spouse who needs to share a feeling. An equally important skill in communicating with one's partner is that of receiving or in listening.

As you learn to effectively listen to and understand what your companion is saying, you may want to consider and take to heart King Benjamin's admonition: "My brethren, all ye that have assembled yourselves together, you that can hear my words which I shall speak unto you this day; for I have not commanded you to come up hither to trifle with the words which I shall speak, but that you should hearken unto me, and open your ears that ye may hear, and your hearts that ye may understand, and your minds that the mysteries of God may be unfolded to your view." (Mosiah 2:9.)

In this prophet's words, we find two essential skills that we can apply to understanding our partner's expression of their emotions. As King Benjamin states, we must first have an attitude of attention and interest—an "I-care-about-what-you-are-about-to-say" attitude; and, second, we must have a desire to listen with the ears, the mind, and the heart, so as to be able to comprehend what our partner is telling us.

When we listen with our minds and hearts, we might first determine if we have heard what our partner meant to communicate. This can be done by asking something as simple as, "Do I hear you saying that you. . . ?"

Once we receive a confirming signal that we are interpreting things correctly, it's much easier to resolve the issue at hand. But it is essential that we provide verbal reinforcement to our partner.

Positive verbalizing, or paying compliments, can be the glue that holds a relationship together. While most of us are quick to comment on the negative aspects of marriage, too often we take the positive things for granted. One author explains:

> The best way one can teach a tongue-tied spouse is by example. Compliments multiply and tend to beget other compliments. Nothing comes across phonier than false praise, so we must be sure to be sincere. On the other hand, many of us need to learn how to graciously accept a compliment with a sincere "Thank you," rather than with a contradiction. Telling our partner how much we appreciate them is a gift that costs nothing, but means everything. Nothing says loving like sincere appreciation. (Diane Halles, "Words that Can Warm Up Your Marriage," *McCalls,* April 1989, pages 70-71.)

It is important to send as many positive verbal messages as possible. Verbal intimacy is achieved when a couple is successful at doing this as well as at sharing feelings of frustration, loneliness, and so forth. The underlying elements of such a relationship is mutual trust and respect, and only when these ingredients are present can a couple achieve true intimacy.

Conclusion

Verbalizing thoughts and feelings is essential to a vibrant, growing marriage relationship. It is perhaps the first type of intimacy a couple experiences as they prepare to become close in other areas.

We hope that the ideas explored in this chapter will assist you and your partner as you further refine your own skills of sharing and caring. Only then can you effectively internalize the other facets of intimacy in your marriage, and thus prepare your relationship to last into the eternities.

2

Nonverbal Intimacy

As one string upon another builds a rope
to anchor the mightiest ship,
One loving act upon another builds ties that bind
well beyond the grave.
(Author Unknown.)

In reflecting on the early days of our marriage, we both remember the Camelot-like beginning we experienced. As two twenty-two-year-olds, we innocently viewed marriage as a destination rather than as a beautiful, though complex and hazardous, journey.

Little did either of us realize, as we wound our way north out of Manti, Utah, toward Salt Lake City and our honeymoon, that five short months later Brent would be activated into the army and would subsequently be sent to Vietnam.

That separation was a difficult one. We were just settling into a satisfying and rewarding marriage routine. But in retrospect, it was a healthy separation. We found that by learning to express ourselves in letters, our love deepened and solidified. We found that writing feelings down on paper, where words were measured and chosen carefully, was a powerful exercise in learning to communicate effectively.

As we now reread those letters, we can see that they forced us to stretch ourselves and our communicating talents. We didn't just share thoughts and feelings, either; as time passed we found ourselves setting more and more goals, in ink. We now realize that this unexpected intrusion into our first year of marriage was most valuable for us in this respect. It allowed us to step back, evaluate our progress as a couple, and then recommit ourselves to the ideals upon which our marriage had been founded.

We now believe that this forced nonverbal stretching early on served as a crucial anchor to our marriage.

Most couples don't have the experience of separating for a season while still floating along on the clouds of their honeymoon. Still, as a couple, you can begin today to enjoy fresh and invigorating air in your marriage by sharing feelings of love in your own way.

Part One

While taking a communications class in college, we learned that 80 percent of all communicating is nonverbal. This being the case, it is clear that there is great power in unspoken messages. A thorough understanding of how to effectively send such messages in a positive way can lead to significantly increased intimacy in marriage.

There are many kinds of nonverbal communication between husband and wife, many having to do with touching, looking into one another's eyes, holding hands, collapsing into each other's arms, etc. We will discuss these nonverbal signals later, but there is another type of nonverbal communication that deserves discussion—simple kindness and sensitivity between husband and wife. Increased sensitivity between a man and woman increases their sense of oneness.

There are basically two types of charitable acts that you can perform to better your relationship with your spouse. First, do things for your husband or wife, thus sending out a clear, romantic signal. Expressing feelings on paper is one way this might be done. A wife could leave a note in her husband's lunch box, in his suitcase when he travels, under a pillow— or even deliver it to his place of employment. A husband might write a letter to his wife and mail it from work, or perhaps write a letter while on a business trip. Because a love note can be reread several times, it can be cherished that much longer.

However if you say "I love you," but do nothing to support or show that love, then your actions are inconsistent with your words. Being sensitive to your spouse's needs, and then doing kind nonverbal deeds for your spouse, gives meaning to your words.

If you are experiencing frustration or disappointment in your marriage, consider the possibility of writing down your feelings. This can be an effective way of expressing yourself, simply because you can choose your words carefully without having to give an immediate response.

Some marriage partners who are confronted with feelings of frustration find it much easier to express deep feelings on paper before talking things out with their spouse. From that point, a conversation on the subject is easier to approach.

In addition, there are many other ways to develop non-verbal intimacy by sending romantic signals. These can be as direct as making your husband his favorite cake or leaving a mint on his pillow; or, for the husband, purchasing a new nightgown for your wife. Or they might be as indirect as polishing your companion's shoes or fixing his or her toothbrush.

The second type of charitable act involves a deeper commitment to intimacy than the first—and that is simply doing things that will lighten the burden of your spouse's daily tasks.

A friend shares the feelings she has about her husband when he demonstrates this type of nonverbal intimacy: "Even without speaking, I have always appreciated how my husband lets me know he loves me. It might sound silly, but some of my most appreciative feelings surface during the middle of the night when he gets up and takes care of the baby. He doesn't do this always, but we take turns, and it lets me know just how much he loves me."

This woman's husband adds: "Never a moment passes in our home but what my wife is silently expressing her love, either to me or to one of the children. Whether it's preparing a meal, washing several batches of clothes during any given day, or simply bringing me a large glass of orange juice, which is my favorite.

"My wife's quiet messages of love seem to exact from me a desire to perform loving acts for her. My favorite is getting

her car washed and then filling the tank with gas before I hand
the keys back to her. Somehow these small acts of kindness
do wonders for our marriage."

Still another woman, in reflecting her appreciation for nonverbal acts of love, states: "Adding to the luster of my diamond
is my husband's increased involvement around the house. This
has come about as he has become more aware of my needs.
He has a personal goal for me never to have to pick up our
vacuum, and he will sometimes even vacuum the family living
area of our home twice a day. He'll employ the younger children to pick up ahead of him, and before I know what is
happening, law and order have been restored to our home.
His helping lets me know that he really does care about me."

About the issue of a husband's involvement in keeping a
home tidy and clean, Margaret explains: "I was recently given
a book written by Don Aslett entitled *Who Says It's a Woman's
Job To Clean?* In quoting from the *Wall Street Journal*,
he states that women who are homemakers spend more than
eight hours a day on house and family work, while women
who are employed outside the home spend as much as five
hours a day. This compares to husbands who spend only an
average of thirty-six minutes per week in helping around the
house.

"I don't share those statistics in a complaining way. I love
being in my home, and I receive a lot of satisfaction from my
full-time job as a homemaker. But I do begin to feel like a
martyr if I am carrying the entire weight of the house on my
shoulders. Husbands would be surprised at the great benefits
of sharing the load.

"Again, Mr. Aslett states, 'Women become warm and playful
when the house is clean, squared away, and running smoothly.'
He then counsels husbands to 'take over some of the work
and you'll have more time to play and be together. She'll be
less irritated and naggy, prettier, a little more likely to believe
that you really do care . . . and you can use your imagination
from there. We'll really make all those macho foreign lovers

sweat when we start making housework an all-American male passion.'

"I'm so glad my husband doesn't think of housework as 'your' job. He has taken *y* out of *your*, and has tried to make cleanliness in our home a team effort. This has given us a deeper meaning to our feelings as well as to our precious moments together."

Part Two

There are many ways to communicate nonverbally, most of which we don't realize we are using. These are more oriented to our interaction as a couple and include our tone of voice, our facial expressions, our body language, and the subtle, pervading mood we have as we interact with our spouse. In many ways, these nonverbal messages are even more important than the actual words expressed in conversation.

Even though we are inclined to consider physical closeness as being a prelude to sexual intimacy, such a closeness can be very fulfilling independent of further intentions. Tender touching has profound power in any significant relationship. There is a closeness that comes from physically touching that can perform miracles, including healing misunderstandings and gaining a closeness and confidence that is crucial to a viable marriage relationship. Many times the magic of touch brings great satisfaction and bonding to both partners.

As an example of the power of nonverbal intimacy, one woman shares: "Because of our busy life-style, my husband and I usually collapse in bed at the end of a day. We love to then catch our breath as we share the events of our day with each other. As we fall asleep, we cuddle up like two teddy bears, and continue to gain strength and reassurance from these hugs throughout the night."

She then becomes more specific: "I love my husband's hands! They are so rugged, yet so tender. I can recall vividly our first date when, for the first time, he reached over and took my hand in his. Now, years later, I love holding hands with him even more.

"In addition to the act of holding hands, I appreciate how my husband's hands show me so much love, with gentle caressing and expression. Then too, I love how his hands are helping hands and reach out to share the work. I also love how his hands bless me with his priesthood power. There have been many times that I just needed a blessing from him to help me make it through a difficult week. My husband's hands show me that he loves me."

One woman shares a letter that she stuffed in her husband's shirt pocket:

> My Dearest Husband:
>
> How very much I appreciate your great tenderness with me. After having been away on a business trip and then returning home, you are so careful to be sure that I enjoy our intimacy. You treat me with such great respect. For me, I am best able to share myself with you after a day of small kindnesses from you—a hug, an expression of appreciation, a kiss after breakfast.
>
> Even seeing you as a wonderful father increases my desire to be one with you—your delightful laughter as you help baby John with his first steps, your careful listening to our teenage daughter's concern over dating, and all the things you do with our other children. You see, I am able to love you so completely because you are such a good man in all areas of your life. Perhaps I could say that the intimate part of our lives is not an event or a simple act—it is a complex part of the very fabric of our lives together.
>
> Thank you for helping me look forward to our loving times by encouraging me, listening to me, appreciating me, and being so honest. I love you more than words can tell.
>
> Yours eternally,

Remember the cartoon mentioned in the previous chapter, "I know we don't communicate . . . it's one of my few pleasures!" This statement is actually false, for we cannot *not* communicate! We are always sending messages, whether it is with our tone of voice, our gestures, our facial expressions, or with our body language. Even the silent treatment says something. We have found that if we do things with a wince and a grudge, feeling all the while as though we are being used, then our message will be loud and clear. On the other hand, if our attitude is one of service with love, it will be received in the same way. There is a universal law which states that "we love those individuals we serve."

Doing for others creates a bond. This is why, as parents, we love our children so much. We love them, not for all they have done for us, but for all we have invested in them. If we think of this law as an equation that will work for us in marriage, we could say that service is a key to loving one another. We can learn to love our companions more as we do little things that please them.

We have found that it is good to verbalize our nonverbal expectations and appreciations. Different people respond differently to nonverbal cues, and it is good to check out what our partner enjoys or doesn't enjoy.

In *One Flesh, One Heart,* Dr. Carlfred Broderick gives examples of couples who appreciate such a tactic. He states:

> I have known women who would melt if their husbands brought them an unexpected box of candy; I have known others who would be offended that their husbands didn't support their attempt to cut down on sweets; and I have known still others who would feel that such a romantic gesture was a sly attempt to deflect their attention from the real issues in their relationship (whatever those might be).
>
> Men are no easier to please. One might enjoy and appreciate his wife's help on a major project, while another would consider her meddlesome. Most men would probably appreciate their wives being more active in initiating sexual activity. Yet some would be offended, threatened, or put off by it. (Deseret Book, 1986, pages 37-38.)

Dr. Broderick concludes with several intriguing questions:

"Have you ever noticed that when couples give each other back rubs, they tend to give the rub they would like to receive rather than the one their partner wants? Thus a husband may give his wife a firm back rub that she finds painful and even intimidating, while she gives him a feathery massage that he finds ticklish and unsatisfactory."

The point is obvious. We should feel so secure in our relationship with our spouse that we can verbalize what we like and dislike, in terms of nonverbal techniques and messages. Then, and only then, can we insure this type of intimacy in our marriage.

Conclusion

The intent of this chapter has been to provide insight into personal nonverbal cues that spouses can give each other to induce greater bonding and intimacy in their marriage. These stimuli occur when a couple interacts and sends nonverbal messages to each other, and when partners choose to perform acts of kindness for their spouse.

We hope that the ideas and personal experiences shared in these pages can assist you in reaching new nonverbal vistas in your marriage. This will occur spontaneously as you think of creative ways to nonverbally express your feelings for your companion. You can create further intimacy whether you have been married just a few short weeks, or whether you have washed each others' clothes and cars for several decades. Expressed consistently, these nonverbal techniques combine to create a bonding that, in turn, introduces an environment of profound trust and security between husband and wife.

3

Physical Intimacy

Women? Ah, women were the stuff of dreams,
made to be loved; and he who could say the reality
was less than the promise was neither lover nor dreamer.
(Louis L'Amour, *The Walking Drum.*)

Part One

The appropriate nature of the basic family unit of husband and wife is clearly and simply set forth in Genesis 2:24: "And they shall be one flesh." While today this is a common cliché, it is nonetheless important as we consider the binding and bonding that takes place as a couple does indeed become one flesh.

There is only one time when two individuals are truly "one flesh." This, of course, is during the act of love, or procreation. During this act, two individuals become so personal and so intimate with each other that they actually become a part of each other. There seem to be at least two results of this personal, sacred moment of oneness. The first is the deepening bond of attachment that is strengthened between husband and wife, and the second is the unique bond of attachment that develops as a mother carries, and then delivers, a child.

Just prior to King Benjamin's death he held a general church conference with his people. Because an angel of the Lord had appeared to him and had told him what his people needed to hear, King Benjamin was well equipped to speak eternal truths to them.

Among other profound truths King Benjamin taught the following: "For the natural man is an enemy to God, and has been from the fall of Adam, and will be, forever and ever, unless he yields to the enticings of the Holy Spirit, and putteth

off the natural man and becometh a saint through the atone-
ment of Christ the Lord, and becometh as a child, submissive,
meek, humble, patient, full of love . . . ." (Mosiah 3:19.)

The whole purpose of this book, and certainly this chapter,
is to give you ammunition that will assist you in putting off the
"natural man" orientation and inclinations in your own marriage.

When our spirit bodies were organized in our premortal
home, we were created by natural laws, being born to our
heavenly parents. As time passed we gained understanding
from these parents. We gained insight into the difference between our limited spirit bodies and our heavenly parents' glo-
rified, immortal bodies. It seems likely that we began to anticipate the time when we would become like them and would
possess the same procreative powers which were theirs.

By making correct decisions at that early hour of our exis-
tence, we were deemed worthy to leave that first home and
venture forth and gain a body. We then had the challenge to
make proper use of this body by learning to serve our Heavenly
Father to fulfill his purposes. In a way, our Father has given
us power over our body functions and reproducing parts as a
mechanism that will help us grow and overcome the natural
man. This growth process has become known to us as the plan
of salvation. Three features of this great plan, as they relate to
marriage, are as follows:

First, as God's spirit children we are to come to the earth
and receive mortal, temporal bodies. While here, we are to
have agency in our actions and in how we use the bodies
granted to us. That is, we become stewards over our own
behavior.

Second, through a proper use of this agency, each of us is
to prepare for an eternal companion and then to select this
companion, thus creating a new eternal family unit.

And finally, with that companion, and under the direction
of the Holy Spirit, each of us has been commissioned to par-

ticipate in perhaps the most sacred experience possible — that of procreating seed after our own kind.

The procreative powers are central to the aforementioned plan. It is through proper and appropriate use of these powers that we create that which our heavenly parents have — an eternal family unit. (This concept is further discussed in D&C 131:4 and D&C 132:15-20.)

Elder Boyd K. Packer has explained, "The experience of procreation is in fact the very key to our being truly happy." ("Why Stay Morally Clean," *Ensign*, July 1972, page 113.) It is the way provided for spirit brothers and sisters to enter this life and thus prepare for an eternal life with a companion and with our heavenly parents.

Elder Packer also says that the procreative power that lies within each of us exhibits two significant features — it is both strong and constant. Knowing the difficulties encountered in rearing children, our Heavenly Father provided these features as a means of motivating us to bring his children to the earth, as without these features many couples would be reluctant to accept the overwhelming responsibilities of parenthood.

The Lord also understood the elements of opposition facing his children in marriage and in life itself, and so he caused the experience of intimacy to be a bonding and unifying one for both men and women. Since this power of procreation is constant, it can serve as a medium for couples to develop, express, and foster delicate and intimate love feelings.

Contrary to much that is conveyed on the screen and in modern "enlightened" literature, the experience of procreation is not intended to be a self-oriented, personal gratification experience. Rather, it is intended to be one where feelings of love, caring, and giving expand and grow within each of us. As a marriage partner, you can no doubt appreciate that when two people have this orientation toward intimacy, they experience the highest and most noble feelings of love and companionship. Then and only then can two really become one and thereby share in the depth of purpose of this experience.

In considering the importance of intimacy in marriage, President Spencer W. Kimball quoted Billy Graham in the April 1974 General Conference:

> The Bible makes plain that evil, when related to sex, means not the use of something inherently corrupt, but the misuse of something pure and good. It teaches clearly that sex can be a wonderful servant but a terrible master: that it can be a creative force more powerful than any other in fostering of love, companionship, happiness, or can be the most destructive of all of life's forces. . . .
>
> God himself implanted the physical magnetism between the sexes for two reasons: for the propagation of the human race, and for the expression of that kind of love between man and wife that makes for true oneness. His command to the first man and woman to be "one flesh" was as important as his command to "be fruitful and multiply." ("Guidelines to Carry Forth the Work of God in Cleanliness," *Ensign,* May 1974, pages 7-8.)

A year after quoting Billy Graham, President Kimball stated: "We know of no directive from the Lord that proper sexual experience between husbands and wives be limited totally to the procreation of children, but we find much evidence from Adam until now that no provision was ever made by the Lord for indiscriminate sex." ("The Lord's Plan for Men and Women," *Ensign,* October 1975, page 4.)

Our premise, then, is that the sexual union is intended for both procreating and giving nourishment and strength to the marriage relationship.

Part Two

Parley P. Pratt stated the following: "The gift of the Holy Ghost adapts itself to all these organs or attributes that man has which are possessed by God, himself. It quickens all the intellectual faculties, increases, enlarges, expands, and purifies all the natural passions and affections, and adapts them, by the gift of wisdom, to their lawful use." (*Key to the Science of Theology*, 1883, page 101.)

Man has the attribute of creating "oneness" with his companion, and that process is governed and orchestrated by the Holy Ghost.

Regarding intimacy in marriage, the sexual union has at times been regarded as a necessary obligation that should be tolerated, that it was the man's right and the woman's duty to repeat this experience. In recent decades, however, there has been much negative reaction to these excessive views.

The result has done more than correct the errors of the past. Like a pendulum swinging too far, society has moved into a period of excessive permissiveness, where sexual intimacy is flaunted and portrayed and abused to an almost unbelievable degree.

It is crucial that we understand the appropriate, even God-given, role sexual intimacy plays, and then stand firm in our convictions rather than allow ourselves to be tossed to and fro with every wind that surfaces on our television and movie screens or in the magazines and books we read. In sum, we need to avoid the extreme views of the Puritan and Victorian eras as well as the hedonistic extremes of our own sexually permissive day. Instead, we should seek after that which is appropriate and eternally exhilarating.

The thirteenth article of faith states that we should seek after that which is "virtuous, lovely, or of good report or praiseworthy." This is true in the sacred area of intimacy in marriage as much as in any other part of life. The important thing for us to remember is that we must sift the wheat from the chaff, retaining only that which is consistent with revealed truths. We should not only gather correct information about sexuality in marriage, but we should avoid or discard incorrect beliefs as well.

Unfortunately, there are members of the Church, as well as members of our larger society, who have naively accepted the belief that the physical part of the body is evil and debasing and as such should be shunned and avoided. This belief dates back to ancient philosophies and continues to exist in several

modern cultures. It springs from the concept that the mind or
the spirit is the more pure or superior part of man, while the
physical body is the seat of evil things such as passions and
corrupting influences.

This belief has led people to want to enhance the mental
or spiritual parts, while avoiding or denouncing moments of
physical fulfillment. From this orientation it is but a short step
to defining the sexual part of man as primarily a part of the
physical body rather than of the spirit, thus labeling sexuality
as being evil, carnal, and undesirable. This belief was incor-
porated into early Christian traditions and has unfortunately
crept into the minds and hearts of some Latter-day Saints as
well.

The view that the physical body is something low, and that
sexuality in marriage is unholy or evil, is incompatible with
revealed truths about the nature of man. The restored gospel
teaches that each of us is a temple (see 1 Corinthians 3:16-17),
and that because the physical body was made in the image of
God, it too is glorious and desirable. We are born innocent
and pure and with a desire to make correct choices. But as we
move through childhood and adolesence and become contaminated by influences of the world, we learn to compromise, and
thereby become fallen.

Then too, evil intentions do not confine themselves to the
physical body. They arise in the heart and mind and spirit, and
then our bodies may become victims of our unrighteousness
rather than being the source of it. In its mortal state, our physical
bodies are subject to a variety of frailties and imperfections.
Still, normal sexual drives and feelings are not in this category.
The Lord gave us sexuality and commanded us to use this
power and process for his eternal purposes. Moroni cautioned
us against viewing good things as evil: "Do not judge that which
is evil to be of God, or that which is good and of God to be
of the devil." (Moroni 7:14.)

To summarize, it is important to seriously consider intimacy in marriage because it is so crucial to the success of

marriage. President Hugh B. Brown, a former member of the First Presidency, has written: "Many marriages have been wrecked on the dangerous rocks of ignorance and debased sex behavior, both before and after marriage. Gross ignorance on the part of newlyweds on the subject of the proper place and functioning of sex results in much unhappiness and many broken homes." (*You and Your Marriage,* Salt Lake City, Bookcraft, Inc., 1960, page 73.)

It is tragic that, despite the crucial nature of this part of marriage, many parents do not educate and equip their children with correct information regarding sexuality. Too many turn their heads away, hoping that in some magical way their children will gather and assimilate this information correctly. This approach invites teenagers to educate themselves, which education, at best, is disjointed and incomplete. In addition, many of us have brought misconceptions from our youth to marriage, and so we retain an incorrect or inadequate perspective of physical intimacy.

Part Three

Several years ago when Brent began his doctoral studies in the area of marriage and family therapy, he was introduced to the writings of Helen Singer Kaplan, M.D., Ph.D., who is a professor of psychiatry and founder and director of the Human Sexuality Program at New York Hospital-Cornell Medical Center. As both a physican and a psychiatrist, she is eminently qualified to teach about the sexual union. This she has done, writing two professional texts, the first of which was titled *The New Sex Therapy.* While this book is written for the professional marriage counselor, it provides some basic and valuable information. If you are contemplating marriage in the near future, or if you've been married for some time, we feel that sharing this knowledge of the sexual response cycle can be helpful to you.

The Cycle of Sexual Intimacy

Dr. Kaplan divides the male and the female sexual response into four successive stages: excitement, plateau, orgasm, and resolution. (See *The New Sex Therapy*, pages 7-33.) Each person experiences physiological, psychological, and emotional changes in each of these four stages, as follows:

The Excitement Stage

Most of the time we are not experiencing sexual feelings. Our minds are occupied with other things such as driving the car, golfing, studying, working, eating, cleaning house, caring for the children, taking care of Church responsibilities, and so forth. Still, every once in a while something happens within us that creates a slight sexual feeling. We may be holding hands at a special moment, or we may touch each other in just the right way, or we may have a prearranged signal that tells our partner we are longing to share our feelings of love in a physical way.

Physiologically, this phase is characterized by the onset of erotic feelings, accompanied by a physical response in men and lubrication in women. In addition, the woman's body changes and enlarges to allow a union to take place.

One of the greatest mishaps in new marriages occurs when a husband, without understanding the need for his bride's physical preparation, expects immediate consumation, thus leaving his companion unsatisfied and emotionally and physically unable to respond. When this usually painful cycle repeats itself often enough, the wife will often feel that she is an object rather than a participant. Thus the grounds for disenchantment are unknowingly laid.

This tragic beginning to marriage is usually due to the different sexual scripts that we bring with us into marriage. That is, we have a preconceived idea of how we want to respond to these feelings of excitement, or intense interest, and our idea or script does not match what our spouse thinks should take place.

In talking about the need for couples to understand and share their preconceived notions, Dr. Carlfred Broderick states:

When a couple feels dissatisfied with (the sexual) part of their relationship, it is extremely helpful to share their sexual scripts with each other. Many couples find it difficult to do this because one or both may view sex as so sacred or so private or so shameful that it is very uncomfortable to discuss in any detail. Nevertheless, it is my experience that a sharing of sexual scripts can provide the awareness needed to solve many perplexing problems in this area. It is like turning on a light in a dark room so that one can see more clearly what the real obstacles to shared satisfaction might be. (*Couples*, Simon & Schuster, Inc., New York, 1987, page 140.)

One couple shares the following about setting the right mood for physical intimacy:

The sexual part of our life is very different at different times. At some times it has been a spiritual experience. When we have been trying to conceive a child we have sometimes felt a kinship with Heavenly Father and have felt that our sexual interaction was almost a heavenly process. We've felt like we were assisting our Father in helping to bring spirits to the earth, and it has been a spiritual feeling that initiates our desire to be intimate with each other.

At other times our intimacy has been a means of sustaining and support. When one of us is low, we love to be close and to be touching with each other. Sometimes we'll snuggle up and lay close to each other for a while, and it is a rejuvenating feeling which may or may not lead to a full expression of our love.

There are other times when our desire for closeness has been born of romantic notions. We sometimes decide days before to have a night of romance, and we make a "date" with each other. As that special time arrives, we may get dressed up and go to dinner, or have a special meal or desert at home, listen to some of our favorite music, and eventually find ourselves sharing love with each other.

We have also found that the intimate part of our marriage is precious after there has been a problem or difficulty between us. When we have had a serious disagreement or a problem between us that has brought tears and hurt and sadness, we find that the concluding act of getting over the problem is to initiate love-making as a healing experience. Somehow this helps us get close together again, and this has become sort of a signal to both of us that there is not discomfort between us.

Our society has taught us that the husband is to be the aggressor, the one who makes the initial advance toward sexual intimacy. From our experience, this is a false and chauvinistic notion. When the wife assumes the aggressor role and shows interest, it is rewarding to both.

If a wife or a husband is romantic and shows that they are desiring affection early in the day, then those desires and feelings build for both partners until evening when the house is quiet and those feelings can be adequately expressed. Anticipation adds fire and emotion to this vital stage.

One couple shares:

> I remember one time when we were going on a trip together. We flew to New York, and toward the end of the flight we found ourselves holding hands and squeezing each other in ways that signaled that we were getting interested in expressing our love. We then had to wait for a bus ride to the hotel, and both of us were so excited that we could hardly stand it. As soon as we could get checked in, we had a passionate and rewarding evening together.

In considering this first stage of excitement, whatever the initial trigger mechanism for romantic expressions, this stage is characterized by the onset of erotic feelings for one's partner.

Like any other emotion, sexual excitement begins as a small feeling. Also, like any other emotion, this feeling can grow and expand until it becomes very intense, compelling and consuming. If you are presently in a healthy, growing marriage, you will appreciate that these feelings are natural for both you and your spouse, and that they contribute to the depth and breadth of your relationship.

The important thing to remember, in summarizing the excitement or sexual arousal stage, is that each partner must feel trust in order to proceed with an expression of intimacy. You've heard the old saying that "you get more with sugar than you do with vinegar." Sugar, or acts of kindness, create a deep and powerful trust between a husband and wife, and this trust is developed by understanding each other's scripts, or each other's expectations, of this most intimate expression of love.

The Plateau Stage

When a couple is adequately aroused, and an intimate expression of love has commenced, a plateau period takes place. Couples usually experience more and more excitement until gradually they reach this plateau, which is accompanied by both partners beginning to focus on this intimate expression while leaving the cares of the world behind. They find themselves experiencing a continual feeling of intense elation and enjoyment.

During plateau, the local physical response is at its peak for both the husband and the wife. While this is true, it is important to understand that there is a very distinct difference in the way the husband and the wife normally respond in the excitement and plateau stages. The man usually moves through the excitement phase more quickly than does the woman. When this occurs he is physiologically and emotionally ready to consummate this act before she is.

If the couple tries to complete the sexual union at this time, it can create several problems. The wife may not be adequately lubricated and subsequently experience discomfort and even pain. In addition, she may not be emotionally ready to proceed, and may therefore resent her husband's attempts to prematurely effect the union. (Remember the disparity in sexual scripts. This is a prime example.) It wouldn't take too many repetitions of this theme for a mutual resentment and frustration to be built up about this most crucial and sacred moment in marriage.

Even if you, as a couple, feel that you understand each other's scripts and that you believe you have great similarity in sexual role expectations, it would be good to periodically discuss your patterns of interacting. As couples move through the various stages of life, their sexual expectations and abilities change; and so by doing this you will learn to respond more adequately to the needs of your spouse. You will continue to love each other in ways that will allow you to move through the natural cycle of becoming aroused and excited, thus preparing your mind, your body, your emotions, and your spirit for the moment of sharing love.

One woman shares her perceptions about this stage: "Tender touch is a very important part of this plateau stage of sharing love. It is the caressing and touching and trying to please your partner that gives you a warm and responsive feeling. One who is thinking of his or her own needs, or who is spectatoring by examining the experience as an outsider, cannot adequately help their partner achieve satisfaction. On the other hand, one who is trying to please their partner, in a righteously unselfish manner, will receive satisfaction back."

Brent says: "If there is one observation I have made during the past two decades of marital counseling, it is that husbands become too concerned with the act of making love and ignore the needs of their wife. Then great apprehensions and inhibitions build up in both of them. I honestly believe that if a woman is treated tenderly and shown concern for her satisfaction, she will open up and desire expressions of intimacy every bit as much as does her husband. Women are emotional creatures, and when a husband positively responds to the emotional needs of his companion, very fulfilling moments of intimacy take place."

When a man is experiencing the act of love, his mind usually has single vision and he concentrates fully on what is transpiring. A woman, on the other hand, often has mental distractions. She may be wondering if Johnny is about to wet the bed, or if one of the children is going to open the door at any moment (all master bedrooms, in homes where children reside, should have doors with locks on them), or if someone remembered to close the garage door. The right romantic setting is very important so the woman can forget the world and be totally, mentally caught up in the sharing experiencing with her husband. The plateau stage can also be portrayed as a time to verbalize one's feelings toward their spouse. As one husband suggests:

> Silence during love-making can be like a wall of ice. I love it when my wife and I talk to each other when we are sharing love. I often hear my wife's words, "I love how you love me." She has told me time and again how she likes to hear me describe how I feel toward her, and what I am experiencing. I also ask her, "What pleases you most?" True fulfillment is reaching out to our partner and trying to fulfill their needs. Often a sweet "Thank you for loving me" is the beautiful conclusion to our expression.

We are now ready to discuss the third phase of sexual intimacy.

The Orgasmic Stage

The orgasmic stage, or culminating moment, is usually the shortest of the four stages of sharing love and seldom lasts more than a few seconds. It is the brief period when the peak of sexual excitement occurs and creates a moment of intense feeling of love and expressions of tender affection for the spouse.

Physiologically, the moment of orgasm has three components for the husband: (a) semi-involuntary muscular contractions in the entire abdominal area; (b) extremely intense and pleasant sensations; and (c) an ejaculation of semen containing up to 500,000 life-producing chromosomes called spermatozoa.

The moment of climax for the wife has two physiological

components: (a) a series of semi-involuntary muscular contractions similar to the husband's; and (b) the same type of
intense and pleasant sensations. The wife's body does not experience anything comparable to the male's ejaculatory response, though her vaginal muscles contract.

While there are many myths about men and women desiring and needing to achieve simultaneous and mutual orgasm,
it is our impression that when a couple knows and understands
each other's sexual scripts, they can provide total fulfillment
for each other. When a couple knows and understands each
other's feelings and needs (as well as their comfort zones),
and when there is mutual trust and respect, the peak physical
response becomes effortless and even secondary. The important thing is that couples talk and verbalize their needs and
expectations.

Perhaps we could share a final thought. A woman does not
always need to experience orgasm in order to achieve total
fulfillment. Nor does her husband. In fact, as a man ages, his
regenerative or refractory period (the amount of time which
must elapse between orgasmic experiences) increases as well.
On the other hand, a woman's ability for peak physical response
increases as she passes through her twenties and thirties. A
man's ability to perform peaks at the conclusion of his teen
years. A love-making session can end without both partners
achieving orgasm and not create great frustration if there is
understanding.

As a couple ages, each partner should be sensitive to each
other's physiological condition and ability. When a person understands the needs and abilities of his or her partner, and is
then sensitive to those needs, the physical act becomes an
expression of love rather than a moment of selfish pleasure-
seeking. The key to fulfillment is providing emotional gratification during this experience, while allowing the physiological
effects to become secondary to the emotional needs of each
partner.

And now for the final stage in the sexual response cycle.

The Resolution Stage

Once emotional and/or physical orgasm takes place, a couple concludes the sexual embrace with a period of gradual reduction in sexual and emotional excitement.

During this stage, the resolution for the husband is involuntary and begins to occur within a few seconds after orgasm. The entire resolution phase for him may be over in a period as short as ten to thirty seconds. He then enters a period of sexual satiation and is unable to physically respond for a period of time.

For a woman, the resolution stage lasts longer than for her husband. It is during this stage that she will experience what is commonly referred to as the afterglow. Her interest in being physically close and romantic may take fifteen to thirty minutes to subside. An abrupt ending on the part of the husband, such as turning on the television or insensitively rolling over and going to sleep, can undo much of the bonding that has just occurred during the sexual union.

It is important that couples understand, and respond with understanding, to this natural difference between the husband and wife during the resolution stage. If it is ignored, it can cause resentment and do ultimate damage to the perceived fulfillment of this experience on the part of each partner.

One woman shares:

> Much has happened, through the years, in my husband's understanding my needs and then responding to them. This is especially true as we conclude a session of intimate lovemaking. I have particularly appreciated the empathy my husband shows to my needs, and the discovery we have made to use these concluding moments of intimacy as a time to share feelings and needs either of us may have at that time. It is usually my needs that are discussed, but lying in each other's arms at that time has given an added dimension to our oneness with each other.

We have discovered that the concluding stage of sharing

love can be one of the most fulfilling moments of intimacy. It can become a time when feelings are shared verbally, where empathetic conversation can take place as one partner seeks to understand how his or her spouse is feeling, and where mutual interests can be discussed.

Dealing With Issues and Setbacks

Shakespeare wrote, "Love is not love which alters when it alteration finds."

We recall spending time with two couples who took us into their confidence. The first of these was a young man and woman who had recently become engaged and were full of hope and expectations. We found that the young woman was anxious about their approaching marriage. Like her fiancé, she had kept herself virtuous and worthy through her years of dating. But, unlike him, she had been fed inaccurate and unfortunate information from her mother regarding the role of intimacy in marriage. Consequently, whenever this couples' wedding date would draw near, she would postpone the date in fear of what the wedding night might bring.

The four of us visited late into the evening, and before long we became insignificant observers as this couple talked openly with each other. Fortunately for this young woman, her fiancé was wise beyond his years, and because he showed great concern for her and empathy about the situation, her fears began to dissipate. The true magic of that evening became evident as the young woman realized, for the first time, that her fiancé was concerned more about her emotional comfort zone than about his own expectations of their wedding night.

Once this young man displayed such sensitivity, the couple proceeded toward their date with destiny. This time their wedding date was kept, and they now seem to be safely and securely launched into their own marriage orbit. There is power in getting started on the right foot. Because fears and expectations were brought out in the open, and then discussed, this couple avoided problems that seemed inevitable.

The story of the second couple is not as happy. This husband and wife wed almost forty years ago. Like the earlier couple, they had remained virtuous until their marriage, which was performed in the temple. Unlike the first couple, they married with little or no discussion about perceptions and expectations of sexual intimacy in their relationship.

Unfortunately, as their marriage began the new husband showed little consideration and sensitivity toward his bride's needs and feelings. The result was all too common: During ensuing weeks and months this young woman developed increasing resentment toward her husband for the way he approached their brief moments of what she began to call mechanical intimacy.

Time passed, and after having several children this lonely and unfulfilled wife terminated any sexual activity with her husband. In her mind she did this out of survival, and she resolved to never allow her husband near her again. Her husband subsequently sought gratification outside their marriage, and he now finds himself without his membership in the Church and without a companion who cares.

This second scenario is, tragically, too often repeated. There are two recurring reasons for this downward spiraling trend. First and foremost is the lack of understanding and preparation on the part of both partners prior to their wedding date. Second, and equally as tragic, is the courtship born of selfishness, a courtship where "making out" and physical gratification dominate the prewedding relationship. This type of behavior tends to accelerate into even greater selfishness after marriage vows are made.

As difficult as such circumstances and patterns are, it is possible to reverse this trend—even after years of marriage. If you and your partner are discouraged and bogged down because of unfulfilling moments of intimacy, we recommend that you make preparations to begin a fast of sorts.

Kneel in prayer and put the intimate part of your marriage on hold. Indicate to the Lord that you will reconsummate your marriage vows after you have determined to share moments of intimacy on a higher, more celestial basis. That is, covenant that from this moment you will not relegate the sacred intimate expression of love-making to having sex. Instead, promise that you will prepare to always share love. "Having sex" in and of itself can be a selfish experience, one that too often doesn't lead to growth and bonding. On the other hand, sharing love can become one of the most unifying experiences a couple can share.

After you have allowed the tension and uncomfortable habits surrounding intimacy to dissipate and leave your bedroom, prepare for your renewal moment by getting away from the children (if there are any still at home) and having a second honeymoon. An alternative is to arrange for your children to visit their grandparents or friends while you stay home alone and rediscover your love for each other.

Finally, remember that when considering this most personal part of marriage, the word *sacred* is paramount. Friends and family members have no right to information about this part of your relationship. The only time it may be appropriate to share details of such a personal nature is if you determine to seek guidance from the appropriate priesthood leader and/or a professional counselor.

Conclusion

Research indicates that the amount of satisfaction a couple experiences in sexual intimacy is directly related to the overall satisfaction they have with their marriage. Physical intimacy is the single most predictive barometer of satisfaction a couple perceives having in their marriage.

Our intent in this chapter has been threefold: first, to discuss how this beautiful and profound facet of intimacy should be regarded — that is, within the sacred framework our Father in Heaven has ordained; second, to provide a detailed statement about the physical process and punctuation marks of love-making; and third, to explore the foundation of a healthy, satisfying physical relationship.

Let us share a final concept that, for us, has been helpful as we have tried to analize how love and trust all fit into our Father's plan for this area of intimacy in marriage.

By the world's standards, the foundation blocks of a happy marriage might be described as being something like this: Happiness leads to communication, which results in sexual fulfillment.

A celestial relationship, however, might be built upon the following foundation blocks: Happiness leads to love, which leads to trust and respect, which results in the fulness of the gospel.

Having a clear and correct perspective about the foundation blocks in marriage makes it easier to insulate ourselves from the worldly definitions of and expectations about physical intimacy.

4

Emotional Intimacy

Love gives itself—
it is not bought.

As important as physical intimacy is in marriage, emotional intimacy—the ability to completely trust and give yourself to someone else emotionally—is perhaps more critical. Emotional intimacy can sustain couples, and in fact any meaningful relationship, if need be, through the most trying of circumstances and across great distances.

Learning to identify and understand our emotions is a lifelong quest. Emotions are fragile, spontaneous, and unpredictable. Even so, those who learn how to be close emotionally will find that an added dimension of bonding or oneness takes place.

Our goal in this chapter is to explore three central themes: emotional health, emotional honesty, and emotional maturity. Partners who learn to deal successfully with their emotions in each of these areas are well on their way to complete intimacy and oneness in their marriage.

Part One

One Friday evening we cornered our eleven-year-old daughter Jennifer and asked her to babysit while we went to the movies. She wasn't thrilled with the prospect of spending a weekend night tending her three younger brothers and younger sister, but she knew that her four elder brothers were nowhere to be found and that she was elected by default. She hesitantly accepted.

It was our night out, and we were anxious to see the movie our eldest son had recommended—*Willow*.

We weren't disappointed in the movie. *Willow* was a story of adventure, but even more it was the story of a man who loved his wife and two children enough to leave them so that he could ultimately provide safety for them. At the conclusion of the story, when the family was reunited, we were both teary-eyed.

As we ordered dinner after the movie, we talked about how kind this husband and wife were to each other. That movie prepared us emotionally to enjoy the remainder of the evening together. It helped us be open with each other, and it set the mood for gentle, sensitive interchange.

In reflecting upon our need to become one, we considered the two different types of love described in Brent's doctoral studies. The first, articulated by a scholar named Winch, states: *"We love those who satisfy our needs."* A differing orientation to love is shared by a family scholar named Prescott: *"We satisfy the needs of those we love."*

The first definition is obviously a selfish one and, in fact, is in direct contrast to the very word *love.* The second definition, however, reflects a more giving, Christlike kind of love and exhibits emotional maturity.

Consider this verse, by an unidentified author:

> *I suppose it was something you said*
> *That caused me to tighten*
> *And pull away.*
> *And when you asked, "What is it?"*
> *I of course said, "Nothing."*
> *Whenever I say, "Nothing,"*
> *You may be very certain there is something.*

That little word *nothing* is a sure signal that something needs to be shared.

Margaret states: "I like to compare the emotional state of marriage to a budding rose. If the bud is kept in a cool room without proper light, it will remain tightly closed and show only two or three of its petals. But if the bud has ample light, water, and warmth, it will blossom in a natural way. Only in full bloom can the beauty of the rose and all its petals be seen. A bud cannot be forced open without damaging its delicate petals. Thus, the process of blooming has to occur naturally and spontaneously.

The rose is much like a marriage relationship.

"Where there is a fear of being ridiculed, or being put down, the cool atmosphere may prevent our companion from opening up and sharing honest feelings. But when this is an atmosphere of warmth and trust, it is much easier and less risky to open up and share emotions. This kind of emotional interchange cannot be forced. But it will happen naturally when the climate is right."

One couple gives this example of being emotionally honest with each other:

> Sometimes one of us wants to make love and the other doesn't. The one who doesn't may be too tired or may just not be interested. For many years in our marriage we struggled with how to "say no" in ways that didn't make the other person feel badly. When that is the case, one thing we try to do is make a date for a later time. We have found this helps the one who was interested to be patient and to not feel unloved or rejected.

While Brent, Wes Burr, and Terry Baker were writing a marriage strengthening program at BYU, they developed a concept that Brent claims is one of the few original ideas he has ever had. Even so, he acknowledges that Wes Burr first articulated the concept, but that he and Terry helped inspire its discovery. The concept is a simple one: *benevolent blindness*.

Brent remembers the day they first centered on this idea. "We talked about the far-reaching implications this idea could have. Terry realized that, while he hadn't had a label for it, his wife, Patti, had been practicing benevolent blindness for years. 'In fact,' he admitted, 'if she hadn't, I'm sure our marriage would have ended long ago.' "

Stated simply, benevolent blindness is the idea that married couples should always be benevolently blind to each other's imperfections.

Brent continues: "One of the things I have appreciated most about Margaret is that she, like Patti, has nearly perfected this notion. She keeps her eyes half closed to my imperfections (leaving them slightly open so that she can see to pick up my dirty socks, if I have forgotten to put them into the hamper, and so forth). And taking things a step further, she doesn't make me pay for these imperfections, whatever they might be. Believe me, her benevolent approach is like magic and works miracles in our marriage."

President David O. McKay once said that we should marry someone who inspires us to grow and improve *at our own choice.* If you are the partner who is practicing "long-suffering" (something that applies to each of us at different times), try quietly encouraging, not nagging, and then pray that your partner will be sensitive to the Spirit and will want to improve in certain ways.

On one occasion we visited with some friends about the concept of benevolent blindness, and the woman, who is very bright and articulate, quipped: "There is another concept couples should incorporate, and that is what I call *discriminatory deafness.* My husband and I have learned that when one of us speaks an unkind word (whether the comment was intentional or not), we try to not take what is said personal. We have often talked of our going deaf to an inappropriately expressed thought or emotion, and we feel it has saved us from a great deal of conflict."

Benevolent blindness and discriminatory deafness, when practiced by both partners simultaneously, can have incredible impact on the quality and satisfaction of the relationship.

Part Two

Though Problems May Arise

There are times for all couples when situations arise that cause emotional pain or discomfort for one or both partners. This is called life. It would be nothing short of impossible for two people from different backgrounds, and therefore different expectations, to join together to traverse the road of life without running into obstacles, roadblocks and hazards that create frustration and pain. While this isn't a startling revelation, unfortunately some couples become resigned to their pain and simply decide to stick it out. They do this because (a) they have made eternal covenants to stay married, (b) they don't want to admit social failure, or (c) they determine to remain in an unsatisfactory relationship "because of the children."

Yet is it reasonable to believe that divorce and tolerance are the only two solutions to a troubled relationship? No. There is another alternative. We call this option *reflective retrenching.* Stated simply, this is the process of getting away from the children for an hour, a day, a weekend, or even longer, if necessary. Once away, a husband and wife are free to consider what is blocking the relationship, what barriers may be inhibiting the relationship, or what is causing the pain-ridden emotions that either or both partners may be experiencing. It is a time to get to the root of the problem without blaming or manipulating each other, and then determining how to remedy the situation.

We have identified several barriers to emotional intimacy that seem to recur in marriages.

Perhaps you are at your wit's end. You may even be contemplating a divorce. Or, maybe your marriage is intact, but you just don't feel a closeness to your partner anymore. Whatever the reason for your despair, the following barriers may help you reverse your collision course and begin your marriage anew.

Barriers to Emotional Intimacy

Barrier Number One

Your marriage has become a flat tire. All of the "air" has gone out of it, and moving forward seems impossible. You feel very discouraged about your marriage and are perhaps even in a state of total despair. There doesn't seem to be much hope.

We suggest to those of you to whom this sounds all too familiar that where there was once air, air can arise again. President Spencer W. Kimball once stated that if two people love each other when they marry (in other words, there is lots of air), and *if they both keep the commandments,* that marriage need never end in divorce.

You can begin to reinflate your marital tire by acting as though there is still oxygen in your marriage. Act as though emotions and feelings of love exist. This cannot be done with a critical eye, but must be done with 100 percent effort on both parts — and, of course, with benevolent blindness. This is not to say that you won't have a bad day once in a while. Rekindling feelings of love is a process, not an event or a commitment. But the commitment to act as though you feel the emotions you no doubt felt during courtship will be a beginning. By being blind to the weaknesses of your spouse, or in your relationship, it is possible to recapture that which was once beautiful and alive.

Professional counselors and marriage advisors refer to a principle known as *Deutch's Law.* Stated simply (and applied to marriage) it is that "the more we act in a certain way, the more our partner will act in that same way."

This law has two components: the ripple effect and the restoration effect. The ripple effect is stated above. The restoration effect comes into play when those around us model our good behavior, thus reinforcing our actions and encouraging us to perpetuate the same behavior.

The more one partner displays loving behavior (even

though that behavior may at first seem awkward and contrived), the more the other partner responds by acting in the same way. This can only cause an escalation of loving emotions and loving events in the marriage.

Barrier Number Two

The second barrier occurs when a person does not feel accepted by his or her partner (which is emotional rejection), regardless of the love displayed and the loving behavior shared.

A feeling of rejection causes some of the deepest pain a person can experience, and it is not easily dealt with. Too often, when a person rejects his or her partner, it is because of personal selfishness and/or unrighteousness.

Selfishness can destroy even what may have been a strong marriage. Couples who are moving forward in their relationship are those who have learned to put in more than they expect to draw out—an attribute that is admittedly challenging to develop and even harder to maintain. But until a husband and wife agree to throw away the ledger wherein they keep track of every misunderstanding and mistake, problems will bubble to the surface. In learning to be selfless, a couple must realize that no two people have the same needs for love and that needs can be met in different ways. Don't make your partner feel guilty when his or her needs are different from yours; neither should you feel rejection when your needs are different than his or hers. Learn to think of your companion— his or her needs, desires, feelings, and so forth—first.

Betrayal in marriage is perhaps Satan's greatest tool in breaking up a once harmonious home. If either you or your partner need to confess an unresolved sin, set up an appointment with your bishop or a member of your stake presidency and get it resolved.

It is tragic to know of the couples who, after years of marriage, determine to finally cut out the cancer that is eating at the foundation of their happiness by confessing an unresolved, and at times premarital, sin or indiscretion. It is amazing how quickly a marriage heals when one or both partners are no longer carrying the burden of transgression.

One of the basic principles of the gospel is agency. Even though it is difficult to continue to endure, some individuals sometimes must live with their pain until their spouse decides to excise his or her own pain — usually through confessing and repenting of former transgressions.

Transgression is not the only cause of rejection. This can also occur when a person feels a gradual reduction of feelings of attraction to his or her spouse. This sometimes occurs when the partner's metabolism changes at midlife and extra pounds, chins and inches appear.

We think of two good friends, a husband and wife, who both put on a few pounds and added some inches as they moved through their early fifties. We remember visiting with this man on one occasion. He remarked that it didn't matter to him how heavy his wife was (even though they were walking together each evening and were making an effort to care for their bodies), but that what was important was their acceptance of each other the way they were.

One friend defines *perfection* as being whoever and whatever his wife is. He applies this definition to all areas of their relationship. What a healthy implementation of benevolent blindness!

Another friend says about her marriage of over twenty years: "In our intimate life, my husband always makes me feel as though I am the most desirable woman ever. He never notices the physical flaws; or if he does, he doesn't mention them. I hope I do the same for him, although he doesn't have many flaws that I have found."

There is much to learn from these couples and from their approach to their changing circumstances. The reward for each of these individuals is that their companions find great satisfaction and fulfillment in marriage because they do not sense rejection or receive criticism from their spouses.

Barrier Number Three

If the romance starts to leave a marriage, there is a tendency, which is also a trap, for a person to begin to dwell on who their partner *isn't.* The experience of one couple illustrates this point.

Several years ago we were living in Arizona. We lived near a beautiful, older couple who had been married for twenty-seven years, only a few of which were spent as members of the Church.

Not long after we had moved into the area, the bishop asked Brent to counsel with this couple (who we'll refer to as James and Dorothy). He indicated that, though they had joined the Church and married in the temple, they were on the verge of a divorce.

Brent began to work with them. He tried everything he knew from his training, and nothing seemed to encourage this couple to want to continue as husband and wife. Finally, just before we were to move back to Utah, Brent got an idea.

He spent the next several evenings on an oil painting of the Arizona Temple, where this couple had been married just a few years earlier. In the foreground Brent painted a large cactus with a glazed donut on one of the quills. He then had the painting framed, took it to their home, and brazenly hung it on their living room wall. They thanked him for the gift, though Brent was sure he saw Dorothy wince as he put the painting on her wall. Then James saw the donut.

"What in the world is that?" he exclaimed, pointing directly to the unusual cactus.

"What does it look like?" Brent countered, enjoying the moment.

"Looks like a donut to me," Dorothy stated, her brow furrowed.

"You're right, Dorothy," Brent replied. "It is a donut, and I painted it especially for you."

"For me?" Dorothy questioned, pointing to herself.

"It's the least I could do," Brent said, pausing to allow their puzzled expressions to linger. "Dorothy, that donut represents James, as seen from your eyes. Up until now, whenever you have thought of James all you have seen is his 'holes.' You've concentrated on all the things he isn't. From now on, whenever you see that donut, you will be reminded to see who he is. Let's consider just a few things. James has not missed a day's work for over twenty-five years. He has never been unfaithful to you. He honors his priesthood as well as any man I have known. I really believe that if you begin to dwell on his attributes, rather than on his weaknesses, your marriage fire will rekindle to its original flame."

Four years passed, and we were living once again in Provo, Utah, where Brent was pursuing his doctoral studies. One Monday evening the doorbell rang. Standing in the doorway were James and Dorothy. No sooner had the door opened than James swooped Dorothy down, planted his lips on hers, and took her breath away in a kiss that lasted for what seemed like hours. After observing this passionate display, we invited them in and learned that, after thirty-two years of marriage, they were taking a second honeymoon.

When asked what had changed things, Dorothy smiled and said, "Why, the donut, of course. It was Brent's crazy donut."

It was hard to tell who was happier, James or Brent. James and Dorothy still show up periodically on our doorstep, always on another honeymoon vacation to Utah.

The moral of the story is clear: Paint donuts on cactus quills. Or, in other words, look for what's *in* your relationship, not what's missing. Cologne and perfume will be purchased in great abundance thereafter.

One woman, after becoming acquainted with the "donut" story, said: "I had a great experience in collecting donuts a few years ago. I got a piece of paper and pen and then began to write down the traits I had grown to love and appreciate in my husband. As it turned out, I filled both sides of the paper. I wrote these traits in my personal journal so that I could save these donuts through time. Then I wrote a love note to my husband and specifically told him what I appreciated about him and why I loved him so much."

We can each go on a donut search, looking for the qualities we appreciate in and love about our mate. When we are intently looking, these qualities become more apparent.

Barrier Number Four

An unresolved negative experience from youth, where either mental or physical abuse occurred, can create barriers to intimacy. It is difficult to understand those parents who betray the trust of parenthood by abusing their children in some fashion. But it happens. And if a person has experienced some form of abuse — emotional, physical, and so forth — during childhood, it is possible for that person to later experience a kind of emotional paralysis during marriage and find it difficult to open up and trust another person in marriage, a setting that demands trust.

One friend explains:

> I don't know when dad began to abuse my sisters and me, but we each carried our own secret into our own marriages. From the time we were little, dad would tuck us into bed. When the lights were out, he would physically abuse us, all the time whispering that we could never tell. And we didn't tell. That is, not until two of us talked one day and shared the distrust we both felt in our intimate expressions that we had for our husbands. I told my sister that I was repulsed by any man's touch, and the conversation went from there.
>
> This was difficult for us to deal with, but we both went back to our husbands and told all. We lived in the same ward, and so the next Sunday the four of us visited the bishop and told him. Unfortunately, dad had died two years earlier; but still we prayed for strength and for his desire to repent.
>
> One of the happiest days for our family took place a year later. After getting rid of all the anger and betrayal, and

after having professional counseling for our own marriages, we went to the temple and had mom and dad sealed for eternity. We each have a sense of peace now, and we are now able to open up and trust in our own marriages. It has been a long road, but for us it has been worth every minute of it.

If you find yourself inhibited in and perhaps even blocking out emotional as well as physical intimacy, perhaps these feelings stem from experiences you had during childhood. Abuse comes in various forms — physical, mental, and emotional. All leave their mark.

If this is the case, go to your Church leader and rid yourself of this guilt. Persons who live with the memory of being sexually abused as a child, for example, usually feel at least partially responsible for and guilty about the experience. Some carry the guilt for years because they didn't know how to stop it once the abusive behavior began.

If some person abused you, you will be doing that individual an eternity-changing favor by also going to their appropriate Church leader and by sharing the misdeed with that religious steward.

While this could be the most difficult decision you will ever make, it is the only way for you to heal and grow, and it is also the only way for the individual concerned to be given the opportunity to repent and move ahead with life.

The payoff for you will be the removal of hatred and anger that you have probably been carrying for years. You will begin to see the person who abused you as having a form of cancer rather than as someone who is evil. The ultimate payoff, of course, will be the enhanced nature of your own marriage relationship.

Barrier Number Five

Another barrier to intimacy can stem from a feeling of distrust from previous inappropriate expectations and/or behavior on the part of your spouse.

Couples often wonder just what is appropriate in terms of the way they express love to each other. The answer is really quite simple, though it requires a prerequisite. In order for a couple to know what behavior is appropriate and within the bounds the Lord has set, both partners must be living worthy of having the gift of the Holy Ghost operate in their lives. If they are worthy of the Holy Spirit, and if they take their relationship to the Lord in prayer, they will be directed in developing an appropriate and celestial intimate relationship.

One of the greatest mistakes individuals make, especially in the area of physical intimacy in marriage, is a year-in and year-out toleration of behavior that is inappropriate or undesirable. If you are unable to convince your partner that you are uncomfortable with your intimate moments, you should feel free to visit your ecclesiastical leader.

When we first married, we pledged to totally respect the feelings and wishes of each other. That commitment has governed the way we interact with each other physically. Your partner does not own you, nor does he or she have the option of taking you somewhere you don't want to go. Love cannot blossom if it is not built upon the foundation of trust and mutual respect.

Barrier Number Six

Closely related to barrier number five, this barrier involves a propensity, usually on the part of the husband, to be involved in pornography. This problem is almost always a leftover from indulgent behavior as a teenager and is extremely destructive — both to the mental wholeness of the individual as well as to the intimacy of the couple.

Pornography can have stifling effects on a marriage relationship. The person so addicted obtains unreal expectations of intimacy in general and of his partner specifically. Pornography addiction can ruin marriage. It's as simple, yet as deadly, as that.

If you, or your partner, suffer from the illness of addiction to pornography, visit immediately with your ecclesiastical leader. There are those who claim that such activity actually enhances marital intimacy. But that is a lie, and is a tool of Satan.

True intimacy will never take place while one of the partners is involved in pornography. Pornography addiction is just that — an addiction every bit as debilitating as some forms of drug abuse. If professional counseling is required, don't hesitate to seek it.

As a caution to the spouse of one involved in pornography, it is essential to know that the use of such literature can lead to a real illness. A supportive, noncritical spouse can be of great assistance in helping someone remove this cancer from their system.

Barrier Number Seven

Another barrier that can impede the progress of intimacy is the feeling that the relationship is not equal — that one partner does most of the giving, while the other does most of the taking.

Brent explains: "I truly think that we men are the weaker sex. We are more inclined to selfishness and to false pride, and we seem to develop the notion that equality is merely a buzz word not really to be taken seriously."

Margaret gives her viewpoint: "Marriage is not equal. I honestly believe that women do have the most difficult roles. That is perhaps why Brent feels we are not the weaker sex — we simply don't have time to get tired or ill. I think that most women understand our differentness and the consuming nature of our tasks. I also think that the thing we value most is *knowing* that our husbands are sensitive to our needs and that they make an effort to lend their support whenever possible, even though their involvement with home and children will probably never equal that of our own."

Someone once said that you cannot tie a knot in a fifty-fifty relationship, and we have found this to be true. While we do not keep score with who does what for whom, we are both aware of trying to meet the needs of the other. Couples who do not make this discovery ultimately find themselves in the rocky and murky grounds of divorce.

There are different seasons in each of our lives. One partner may carry a greater load, from time to time, in the relationship.

We have often joked about titling one of the chapters of this book "Equally Yoked or Eternally Choked." We haven't, though, because we know that unless a couple develops equality in their relationship there is no eternal choking, for the relationship will not exist past the grave. We have each been reared differently and have had different role models. As a result, each of us must be willing to learn, to look, and to listen to each others' ways. We then need to work together to form our own working models that are equally fulfilling to each of us.

Barrier Number Eight

A barrier develops when we maintain a marriage on a superficial, exchange basis. Too many couples who are struggling to survive keep score and give only when they receive. In addition, some individuals perform loving acts for their partner simply to prove they are better, or to store up points to be reserved for the next disagreement.

The partners who limit their relationship to an exchange of this nature never experience altruistic acts of love. They never allow charitable or Christlike acts to surface, and so their relationship is not allowed to deepen and take root in the fertile soil of charity, empathy, and love.

The following demonstrates this point:

> Has our marriage ever changed! Several years ago, when I was on the verge of leaving my wife and our three beautiful children, we decided to get away for the weekend and make the decision once and for all what our future would be.
>
> We arranged for a babysitter, spent several silent hours

driving to who-knows-where, and finally stopped for the night. Our dinner at the restaurant was likewise silent, with each of us thinking about how poorly our companion treated the other in our marriage.

When we got to our room, we sat down around a table and in the next four hours we experienced most, if not all, of the emotions known to man. We learned more about each other, and the way we had treated each other, than either of us had previously known.

The bottom line came when I asked my wife why she always had a string attached to our being intimate. She surprised me when she said that her string was her only defense, that she thought I wasn't really concerned about her as a woman, but just someone to be with. We then talked about how we were always having to get something in order to give something. And finally, realizing that we had built our marriage on a very shallow foundation, we both decided to repent. At that moment we slipped to our knees, vowed to not keep score with each other again, and resolved to make our marriage work.

And it has worked. We are now totally immersed in each other's love, and we get a very queasy feeling whenever we think of how close we came to losing each other and the family we have now reared.

Barrier Number Nine

Sometimes dutiful wives strive to be such super wives that they rob the husband of equal status in the home, thus causing the husband to become emotionally paralyzed in the relationship.

Male paralysis sets in when a husband is so doted on that he feels unwelcome to participate in the home life. For instance, the wife sees to it that her husband always comes home to a clean house and delicious meals. The children are under control, and she always manages to greet her husband with a big smile and a passionate kiss.

We're not suggesting that the woman should not make her husband's pathway bright when he returns from work each evening. What we are suggesting is that when a woman successfully plays the role of the perfect homemaker, resentment can build in the husband's mind as he begins to feel like an intruder, unable to pitch in and be part of the daily household activities.

A friend of ours told us about her experience. She supported her husband through law school, worked full-time for years, and yet always saw to it that he had the red carpet treatment when he returned home each day. This unintentional "over-doting" began to grate on him until finally they separated and planned for divorce. Luckily, a short time later they realized what the problems were. They are now back together, with the husband contributing to the Cub Scout activities, the lawn care, and any other activity he has time for.

This woman reflects:

> For years I assumed all of the domestic responsibilities, thinking that I was providing the perfect home for my husband. He began to emotionally withdraw, however, until we found that we had little to share with each other. We both thought our companion had lost their love for us, and so we agreed to a trial separation.
>
> During our separation we discovered that I had actually wedged my husband out of feeling a part of our home. We have a lot of habits to break, but we are now in the process of rediscovering our love for each other.
>
> As an example of how I now treat my husband, I might tactfully (and I hope with the right timing) ask him to put the groceries away after we have been shopping. I have learned to simply say, "Thank you, dear" after he has completed the task rather than saying, "Thank you, dear, for helping me." The "helping me" phrase somehow caused my husband to think he was being asked to do something that was really not his responsibility, and that in fact he was doing me a favor. I now feel more secure because I know my husband cares and loves me because of his efforts, and he feels good about his involvement because I have allowed him to contribute to the relationship. That, to us, is the crux of making a true intimate relationship.

Barrier Number Ten

We don't always recognize that being equal is not the same as being the same. A feeling of emotional equality must exist in marriage if that marriage is to last beyond death. Even so, men and women are not the same — and complimentarity is valid and healthy.

Not long ago Brent was reminded of the words to a Neil Diamond song:

> *She was morning, and I was night time.*
> *I was lonely, in need of someone —*
> *You are the sun, I am the moon,*
> *You are the words, I am the tune — play me.*

While the world is shouting about how men and women are the same, it's nice to hear words that echo truth. A solid marriage relationship is one that is complimentary in nature, where the expectations are different from each partner. Both are half of a wheel, and by becoming one whole are able to move steadily forward, always discovering new and exciting horizons in their marriage.

Conclusion

We don't claim that this listing of "barriers" is all-inclusive. But we hope these concepts may give you guidance in understanding the things that can limit the intimacy you achieve with your partner.

If, after working with your partner (and your bishop if necessary), there are issues that you are unable to resolve, we suggest that you contact a professional marriage counselor. Seeking counseling is not an admission of failure, and whether it be for refining your methods of communicating or dealing with severe sexual problems, counselors are equipped to provide valuable and timely assistance. If you feel that you simply can't afford the fees of a counselor, let us suggest that perhaps you can't afford not to afford to see one. It could be one of the most significant phone calls you will make.

Emotional intimacy in marriage creates oneness; and being "one" allows intimacy to flow naturally from the fountain of spontaneity. Being in love is not an adequate license for intimacy, but being physically and emotionally intimate, within the bounds the Lord has set, is a vehicle that leads to knowing and understanding true love.

5

Spiritual Intimacy

*"I say unto you, be one; and if ye
are not one ye are not mine."*
(D&C 38:27.)

We have often thought that one of the greatest kinds of
"hell" we could experience beyond the grave would be to have
the memories of a loving relationship and yet be powerless
to express our feelings or enjoy that relationship any longer.
How painful it would be to not be sealed as one, but to be
eternally alone, simply because we did not invest enough in
our marriage, and in our own personal quest for integrity, to
ensure this relationship into the eternities.

Margaret relates an experience that illustrated this concept:

> Several months ago Brent accompanied his brother,
> Blaine, on a business trip to West Germany. They said it was
> purely business, although Blaine's wife and I knew they
> would spend much of their time exploring and visiting (we
> smiled when they called their trip "researching").
>
> We were lonely wives for nineteen days and nights, and
> eagerly awaited their return. Brent had one experience dur-
> ing the final week that will set the stage for the point we
> are making. He wrote in his journal the following: "We
> journeyed southeast to Munich and to a small town on the
> outskirts called Dachau. Here we spent the night, eager and
> yet also anxious about our upcoming tour of the infamous
> World War II Nazi prison concentration camp.
>
> "On our way to Dachau, I opened a new book I had
> purchased for the trip. It was Elder Neal A. Maxwell's book
> *Meek and Lowly.* On page two, Elder Maxwell refers to the
> question, What think ye of Christ? He then states that in order
> to encounter the abundant experiences of life, we must strive

always to be like Jesus. This transformation takes place when His yoke is placed firmly upon us.

"Reading these words, and thinking about charity, I closed my book and prepared, with Blaine, to drive up the hill to the former concentration camp.

"When we arrived and walked between the wired cement walls that marked the entrance of that former satanic bastian, we experienced a darkness of spirit that was not only unexpected, but was of a forboding magnitude unlike any feeling either of us had ever before known.

"We spent several hours there, reading and learning firsthand the atrocities that Hitler, one of the world's true archenemies to Christ, had committed against those prisoners, almost all of whom were Jews.

"As we saw pictures of the prisoners, and of their bodies being wheel-barrowed off to the incinerators, we couldn't help but reflect on how many of these human beings had spent their final years away from their companions and loved ones.

"Our thoughts then turned westward, to the United States and to our homes in Utah, and we longed to be near our companions. We felt a closeness with them that Sunday morning, an intimacy if you will, that we are still unable to articulate. We discussed how we felt that their spirits and ours were as one, even though we were thousands of miles apart."

Part One

Elder Jeffrey R. Holland discussed the facet of spiritual intimacy in an address given while serving as president of Brigham Young University. The title of his talk was "Of Souls, Symbols, and Sacraments."

In his remarks, Elder Holland focused on one of the eternal truths of the Restoration—that "the spirit and the body are the soul of man" (see D&C 88:15). He then stated that when we consider sexual intimacy as merely a physical experience, we "cannot receive a fulness of joy" (see D&C 93:34).

He explained: "I would also suggest that human intimacy,

that sacred, physical union ordained of God for a married
couple, deals with a symbol that demands special sanctity. Such
an act of love between a man and a woman is—or certainly
was ordained to be—a symbol of total union: union of their
hearts, their hopes, their lives, their love, their family, their
future, their everything. It is a symbol that we try to suggest
in the temple with a word like *seal*." (Jeffrey R. Holland and
Patricia Terry Holland, *On Earth As It Is In Heaven*, Deseret
Book Co., 1989.)

Margaret reflects upon one of the crucial turning points of
our relationship, which is similar to the one shared earlier in
this book: "Though this experience is sacred to us, we feel it
is appropriate to reflect for a moment on our first night as
husband and wife.

"As we prepared to retire, we knelt in prayer so that our
Heavenly Father could be included in our marriage. We held
hands, and my husband offered our first family prayer. In it,
he thanked the Lord for the preparatory sealing that had taken
place in the Manti Temple earlier that day. My heart swelled
as I listened to his words, savoring the memories of our marriage ceremony. He next invited the Lord to bless us with His
spirit, especially in our moments of intimacy. We then pledged
to never abuse this power, but to always elevate this expression
to its intended lofty and sacred position so that one day our
marriage would be sealed by the Holy Spirit of Promise."

As we reflect upon our own union, and the desire we share
to be sealed together throughout the eternities, our hearts beat
with a quiet elation that we have come to rely upon. Like all
couples, we experience moments of frustration, usually re-
sulting from a poor effort at communicating. But still our daily
goals reach upward, with a firm resolve not to allow Satan,
with his telestial enticements, to penetrate our armor of resolve.
Unfortunately, Satan has penetrated at times, causing us pain
and heartache in the process. We have come to view the quest
to free ourselves of his influence as perhaps our greatest challenge, and yet one that, for us, appears ever more attainable.

Part Two

We would now like to move forward two decades from the time we were married and share an experience that took place one early morning with our nine children gathered around us in our living room.

It was May 1987. Our family had been studying the Book of Mormon, and we were finally in 3 Nephi, where we were studying the appearance of the Savior to the Nephites.

Brent remembers that morning: "As we read 3 Nephi 13:22-24, my entire being was affected. Even though I had read and even taught those verses many times before, still they had not impacted my soul as they did that morning. I realized, as we reread them, that the Savior was providing the key for us to become one with him.

> The light of the body is the eye; if, therefore, thine eye be single, thy whole body shall be full of light.
>
> But if thine eye be evil, thy whole body shall be full of darkness. If, therefore, the light that is in thee be darkness, how great is that darkness!
>
> No man can serve two masters; for either he will hate the one and love the other, or else he will hold to the one and despise the other. Ye cannot serve God and Mammon. (3 Nephi 13:22-24.)

"I realized, as we pondered upon these words, that the Savior was in fact providing the key to true righteousness — that being our ability to control our eye. This was the first time that I understood darkness to be a type of light. I had previously considered darkness to simply be an absence of light. Now I knew, as never before, the dark and controlling power of the adversary."

As we have considered this passage together, we have seen more clearly the process of becoming one, or enjoying spiritual intimacy with each other and with Christ. If we allow ourselves to have single vision, by only letting the right type of light into our eyes, we will become filled with His light so that we begin to radiate His countenance. For us, this has affected some of our behaviors. For example, we have made a commitment to never view soap operas or other television programs that might invite darkness, excessively violent or suggestive movies, reading materials that pollute, and so forth. This is essential *if we desire to one day be adopted as Christ's children and thus acquire His attributes.*

Brent had an experience that has made us even more aware of the need to keep our eyes pure and filled with light.

"Not long ago I was quite ill, and I spent three days in bed. Because I was too feverish to read, I decided to conduct a television soap opera survey. I spent three days watching segments of each of the soap operas, keeping a record of each inappropriate behavior that was either discussed or displayed during those programs.

"While I won't share the statistics, I will say that, with the exception of denying the Holy Ghost (which, of course, those media producers were incapable of portraying), every sin that I have knowledge of was shown at least once during those three days. The most profound, and most often duplicated, of course, were the images of immorality that were cast, and the superficial and shallow definitions and displays of 'love' and 'intimacy.'

"I learned even more about my own spirit at the conclusion of this near deathbed study. In just three days I had become totally involved in the storylines of several of the soaps, and I had lost almost all my desire to pray. This made me realize how greatly we are influenced by our environment and how easy it is to be contaminated by the not-so-subtle enticements of our amoral society."

Margaret says: "This experience of Brent's, coupled with other television moments we have had in our home, has caused me to think that often the blue light emitted from a television set is not uplifting. Whenever we, or our children, aren't selective about what we watch on television, our level of spirituality is negatively impacted."

We read in 4 Nephi 1:17: "There were no robbers, nor murderers, neither were there Lamanites, nor any manner of -ites; but *they were in one, the children of Christ, and heirs to the kingdom of God.*"

In D&C 93:2 we read: "I am the true light that lighteth every man that cometh into the world." And from D&C 50:24: "That which is of God is light; and he that receiveth light, and continueth in God, receiveth more light; and that light groweth brighter and brighter until the perfect day."

Margaret remembers talking with a friend who tearfully unloaded the problems in her marriage—primarily, her discomfort with the way her husband was treating her. "My first thought was, 'Have you prayed for him? He must be so disappointed with himself, and so unhappy.'

"I then told my friend I felt that praying for one's spouse and their success and happiness not only helps them, but also helps the person praying be more aware of how they can help their companion achieve their goals. Even though the results may not be immediate, our own spirit will mellow and we will respond much differently to our companion. The result, of course, is that we will be more likely to have the true spirit of charity towards our companion."

It is impossible to attain righteousness as a couple until both partners have made a commitment of personal integrity. Such a commitment is not easy to make, for each of us carries a protective pouch of sins, and the sins contained in this pouch almost become sacred unto themselves.

Once a person determines to toss away this pouch and begins trying to keep all of the commandments, couple unity skyrockets. Relationship righteousness then follows, allowing husband and wife to progress as a unit "until the perfect day," where a couple can enjoy total spiritual intimacy.

We are familiar with several couples who have found that, on occasion, there is a simple but special way to create an intense feeling of spiritual bonding between husband and wife. These couples acknowledge that the physical intimacy they share with each other has different qualities at different times. Sometimes it is very passionate, sometimes tender, sometimes healing. And at times it is particularly sacred. All are good. All work together to create oneness. These couples acknowledge that, at times when it seems appropriate, they have culminated the physical experience on bended knee and expressed gratitude for their marriage and hope for the ultimate eternal bonding that can and will come as their marriage is sealed by the Holy Spirit of Promise.

Indeed, the crowning facet of intimacy is spiritual, where true oneness flourishes. The other four facets of intimacy seem to build upon and work toward being intimately in touch with each other's spirit, and then with the Spirit of our Savior.

One way for a couple to increase their level of spiritual intimacy is to regularly attend the temple together. Great strength comes into the relationship as couples partake of the blessings and spirit found therein.

Attend the House of the Lord often so that you can insulate yourselves from the cares and sins of the world. It is the best place to develop an intimate and eternal relationship with the Savior.

Elder Bruce R. McConkie has written much about the process of becoming Christ's friend. He suggests that there are two personal applications we can make with the Promised Messiah:

> As believing saints, it is our privilege:
>
> 1. To enjoy the gift of the Holy Ghost; to receive personal revelation; to possess the signs that always follow true believers; to work miracles; and to have the gifts of the Spirit; and
>
> 2. To see the Lord face to face; to talk with him as a man speaketh with his friend; to have his Person attend us from time to time; and to have him manifest to us the Father. (*The Promised Messiah*, Deseret Book Co., 1978, page 571.)

It is our impression that believing Saints are those who do more than attain a personal recommend. They are those who earnestly seek personal revelation for themselves and for their family, and who then prepare themselves, with their companions, to see the Lord face to face and thus become his true friend. After all has been said, this would appear to be the most beautiful and intimate moment of all.

Conclusion

It is our hope that, by having shared our personal thoughts and feelings (as well as the tender expressions of friends who have assisted us), you will have increased courage and resolve to create the element of intimacy, or oneness, in your marriage. It has not been our intent in this book to portray ourselves as having "arrived," for we have not. The experience of writing this book together and focusing on the five areas of intimacy in our own marriage has helped us feel a great oneness.

King Benjamin's admonition at the conclusion of his address is relevant for us today. He charged that we live the type of life that will ultimately allow the Savior to "seal us his," which in turn will provide the opportunity for us to share the eternities with our chosen companion, as well as with our children and theirs. Perhaps this is what the Lord meant when he spoke to the Prophet Joseph in the Liberty Jail on March 20, 1839, as recorded in D&C 121:46: "The Holy Ghost shall be thy constant companion, and thy scepter an unchanging scepter of righteousness and truth; and thy dominion shall be an everlasting dominion, and without compulsory means it shall flow unto thee forever and ever."

What a marvelous prospect, having an everlasting dominion (or family) promised to us. It is then that we can rejoice in being identified as sons and daughters of Christ. Truly it is by adhering to the light and way of the Savior that the way is provided for true intimacy to be shared and enjoyed into the eternities.